C O
O L

THE COOLEST THINGS UNDER THE STARS. AND THE SUN.

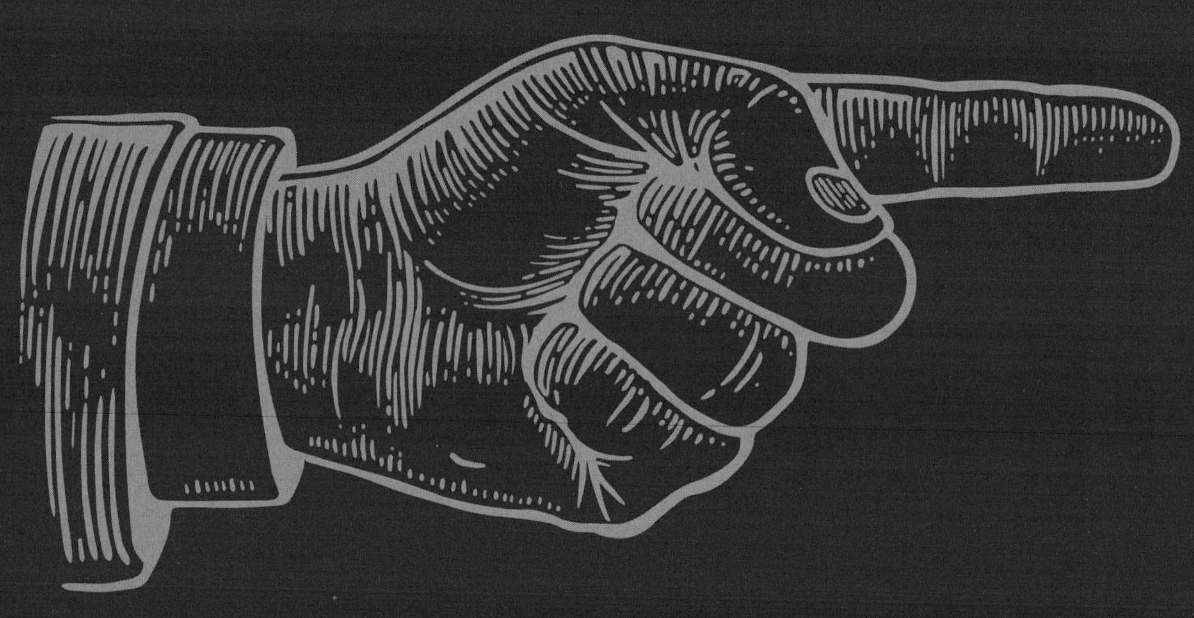

COOL

SWAPAN SETH

PHOTOGRAPHS BY ROHIT CHAWLA

Simon & Schuster

First published in India by Simon & Schuster India, 2023

1 3 5 7 9 10 8 6 4 2
Simon & Schuster India
818, Indraprakash Building,
21, Barakhamba Road,
New Delhi 110001.
www.simonandschuster.co.in
Paperback ISBN: 9789392099984
EBook ISBN: 9789392099960

Typeset by Avanti Talwar
Printed and bound in India by Replika Press Pvt. Ltd.

For Srey: My coolest decision.

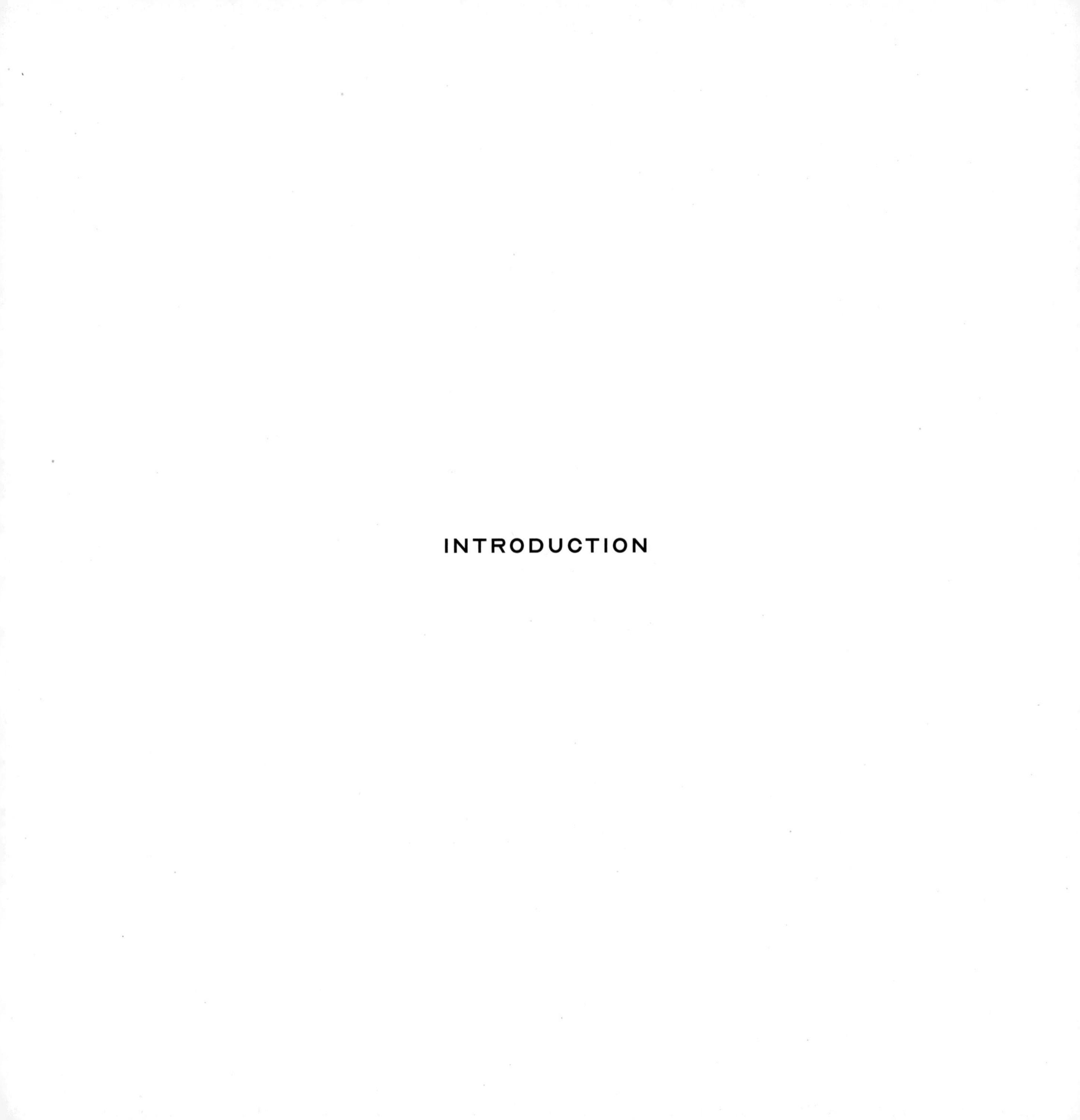

INTRODUCTION

In his brilliant piece written years ago, David Skinner wrote, "Cool is still cool." The word, the emotional style, and that whole flavour of cultural cachet remains ascendant after more than half a century.

It is, according to linguistic anthropologist Robert L. Moore, the most popular slang term of approval in English. Moore says cool is a counterword, which is a term whose meaning has broadened far beyond its original denotation.

Around the 1930s, cool began appearing in American English as an extremely casual expression to mean something like "intensely good". This usage also distinguished the speaker, italicizing their apartness from mainstream culture.

As its popularity grew, cool's range of possible meanings exploded. Pity the lexicographer who now has to enumerate all the qualities collecting in the hidden folds of cool: self-possessed, disengaged, quietly disdainful, morally good, intellectually assured, aesthetically rewarding, physically attractive, fashionable, and on and on.

Years later, "cool" is still that: off centre, moored far away from the mainstream, yet midstream, in a sense. In the game but more spectatorial. A perspective. A snoot. Not a snot.

Cool to me is also utterly democratic in its political purpose. I have a theory that three things have come to define cool across the world. Across ages. Across stages. Think about it. From the hellishly hip streets of Helsinki to the staggering slopes of Spiti, three things unify us: our backpacks, our sneakers, and our earpieces. Cool skips across borders like a carefree child. It swaggers down streets. It is oblivious. That is cool. It's not a well-dealt hand. It's the middle finger.

All my life I have surrounded myself with cool people. Not just young but people with a bent of mind that is just that—bent. People who have conformed to a nuance. Not prisoners of the collective stance.

I have lunch with cool people. I write to them asking them about what's cool. And at the spine of cool is that nerve called curiousity.

Speaking of nerves, cool is much like the Vagus nerve of the body. The word "vagus" originates from the Latin word for wandering. The fact is that cool keeps wandering. It slips from one restaurant to another. From one city to another. And therefore it demands ample attention and amendment.

This book is a compendium of what I think is cool in 2023. From the books to the restaurants to the music to the stocks. Evidently, much of it will change with every passing year.

Finally, who am I to write this? Just a plain purveyor of cool.
Its devoted student. An unabashed fan, maybe.

Several years ago, I wrote an advertisement for a music channel.
The headline said, "I am not the voice of God.
I am just his DJ."

I am just cool's DJ.

I very much hope you enjoy the music.

Swapan Seth

New York

June 2023

CONTENTS

CHAPTER ONE

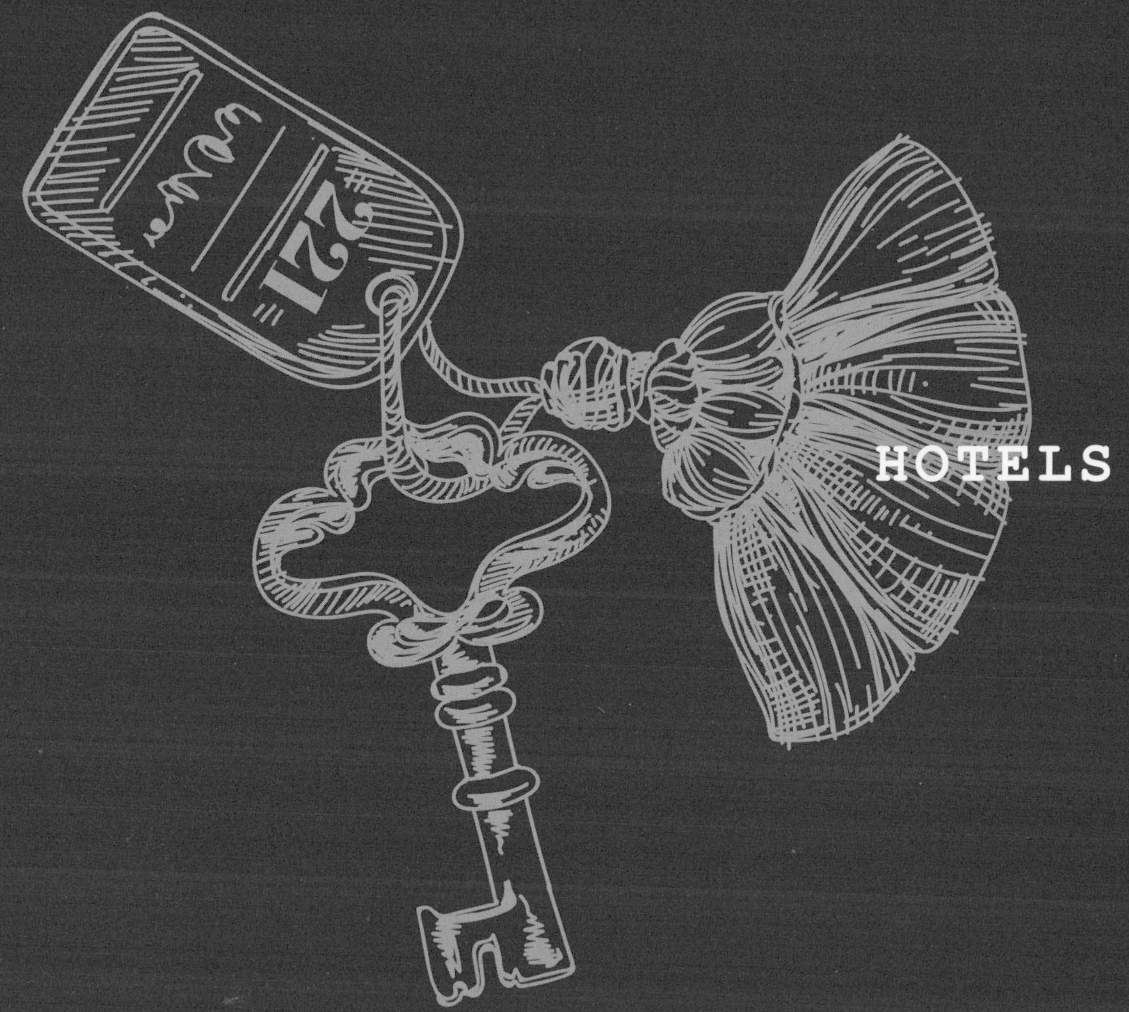

HOTELS

“I have never been a believer in uber-fancy hotels per se. I look for uber-chic stays. The list mirrors that. Some of the hotels in this list have no room service, fixed meals and no in-room dining. But the atmosphere is electrifyingly eclectic and almost always engaging. Others sparkle with great food, scintillating splendour and little thoughtful touches. These are bolts that float my boat.”

>

SITLA ESTATE, MUKHTESHWAR

>

THE AMAN, TOKYO

>

THE POSTCARD DEWA, THIMPU

>

THE METROPOLITON APARTMENTS, LONDON

>

FOUR SEASONS, LONDON

>

GRESHAM PALACE, FOUR SEASONS, BUDAPEST

>

THE RITZ CARLTON, TORONTO

>

ST. REGIS, DUBAI

>

SONEVA FUSHI, MALDIVES

>

THE TAJ MAHAL, MUMBAI

>

LAKE PALACE, UDAIPUR

>

THE THIEF, OSLO

>

THE PIERRE, NEW YORK

>

SHER BAGH, RANTHAMBORE

>

FOUR SEASONS GEORGE V, PARIS

>

THE RAFFLES, SINGAPORE

>

MANDARIN ORIENTAL, HONG KONG

>

NADESAR PALACE, VARANASI

>

THE PARK, KOLKATA

>

TAJ FORT AGUADA, GOA

CHAPTER TWO

RESTAURANTS

I have the palate of a chameleon. It effortlessly changes yet is painfully predictable. As far as possible, I stay away from the fancy and the plain pretentious. I am perfectly at peace with a fine carpaccio as I am with a well-made anda tadka from a dhaba. So, Michelin stars are a red flag. Not because the food is not fabulous but the environment and the portions can get very daunting. I am also a creature of both habit and dishes. And I seldom order from the menu. The restaurants below almost always feed me what I fancy. Which is why, I fancy them.

>

GOLDEN DRAGON, MUMBAI

>

THE TABLE, MUMBAI

>

DEL FRISCO, NEW YORK

>

DIMSUM PALACE, NEW YORK

>

HIDE, LONDON

>

QUILLON, LONDON

>

CAFE DALI, NEW DELHI

>

DELHI CLUB HOUSE, GURGAON

>

EBISU, GURGAON

>

PIZZERIA DA SUSY, GURGAON

>

ABSOLUTE THAI, GURGAON

>

FRANGENTE, MILAN

>

JAAN, SINGAPORE

>

NU VARIETY, KOLKATA

>

RUSSELL STREET DHABA, KOLKATA

>

BAR B QUE, KOLKATA

>

COALESCE, GURGAON

>

EDEN PARK, BENGALURU

>

SCHONNEMANN, COPENHAGEN

>

RATAN'S, PARIS

MIAMI
BEACH'S
CONTEMPORARY
ART
MUSEUM
Ruinart
Ruinart

CHAPTER THREE

WINES & SPIRITS

“

I do not understand wines. I haven't even drunk one. But I am married to a lady who enjoys them immensely and I have fastidious friends who would cringe at something worthless. Having said that I can sip a wine and tell schlock from superb. While it is very simple to bite the bait of a Bordeaux or the cunningness of a Chianti, I prefer to stick to new world wine mostly. The ones from Australia or Napa Valley. Why, even Lebanon. Even when it comes to spirits, I stay away from what's in vogue. So, not for me the tiresome Beluga or unimaginative Botanist. And I would not be caught dead serving Kristal champagne. It is so new-money.

”

>

KOSTA BROWNE

>

TORBRECK

>

CHATEAU MUSAR

>

SANDHI

>

KRSMA

>

CHATEAU FAYAT

>

CATTUNAR

>

HABIT

>

VINO NOBILE DI MONTEPULCIANO

>

NESIOS

>

KYRO, GIN

>

BLACK COW, VODKA

>

YAMAZAKI 18 YEARS, WHISKEY

>

RUINART, CHAMPAGNE

>

MADRE, MEZCAL

>

FRAPIN, COGNAC

>

MOUNT GAY BLACK BARREL, RUM

>

ITALICUS ROSOLIO DI BERGAMOTTO, LIQUER

>

CHIMAY, BEER

>

CASAMIGOS, TEQUILA

CHAPTER FOUR

STORES

I love retail therapy but in places that are tastefully therapeutic. So not for me the gargantuan Harrod's or the insipid ION Orchard. I find my joy in little nooks where I can buy all the things that I fancy from incense sticks, inks, paper, rubber bands, shirts to even sea salt. My go-to-stores are mostly stores that few people have heard of, leave alone visited. They are far away from the high street. More in the by lanes. Utterly missable due to subdued signage but not to be missed because of the beautiful things that they store. I mean, who would have thought that the most fabulous homeware store on this planet is tucked away in a leafy lane in Kolkata.

>

TULA, KOLKATA

>

NILA, JAIPUR

>

VIS A VIS, DELHI

>

HAY, COPENHAGEN

>

LABOUR & WAIT, LONDON

>

TABIO, LONDON

>

DESIGNER'S GUILD, LONDON

>

CULINA, SINGAPORE

>

DONGPOKH, HONG KONG

>

DOVER STREET MARKET, NEW YORK

>

JAMES PERSE, NEW YORK

>

THE MOMA DESIGN STORE, NEW YORK

>

CAPITOL MALL, SINGAPORE

>

LA SIRENUSE SHOP, POSITANO

>

GINZA SIX, TOKYO

>

GAYSORN PLAZA, BANGKOK

>

THE LIGHTHOUSE, DUBAI

>

KAMP GALLERIA, HELSINKI

>

BULY 1803, PARIS

>

RARE MARKET, SEOUL

CHAPTER FIVE

ARTISTS

"

Art is an impossible canvas to curate. More so when one looks at art from all over the world. Now the truth of the matter is that personally, I believe that Indian art is increasingly getting bereft of great ideas. But amidst these dark clouds there are several silver lines. So, my list of cool artists is contained to artists from India or of Indian origin. More importantly, I am also a firm believer that art must not be only the prerogative of the platinum card bloke. Indeed, all of these artists are wonderfully priced and pregnant with promise.

>

AASHNA JHAVERI

>

LATIKA NEHRA

>

AMRIT PAL SINGH

>

MARTAND KHOSLA

>

RATHIN BARMAN

>

SUCHITRA GALHOT

>

TANYA GOEL

>

PARUL GUPTA

>

ROHIT CHAWLA

>

KUNEL GAUR

>

SEHER SHAH

>

AYESHA SINGH

>

SHRISHTI RANA MENON

>

BIRAAJ DODIYA

>

NEERJA KOTHARI

>

SANGITA MAITY

>

PRIYANK GOTHWAL

>

AMIT MADESHIYA

>

KIRAN SUBBAIAH

>

PARUL JESUDASAN

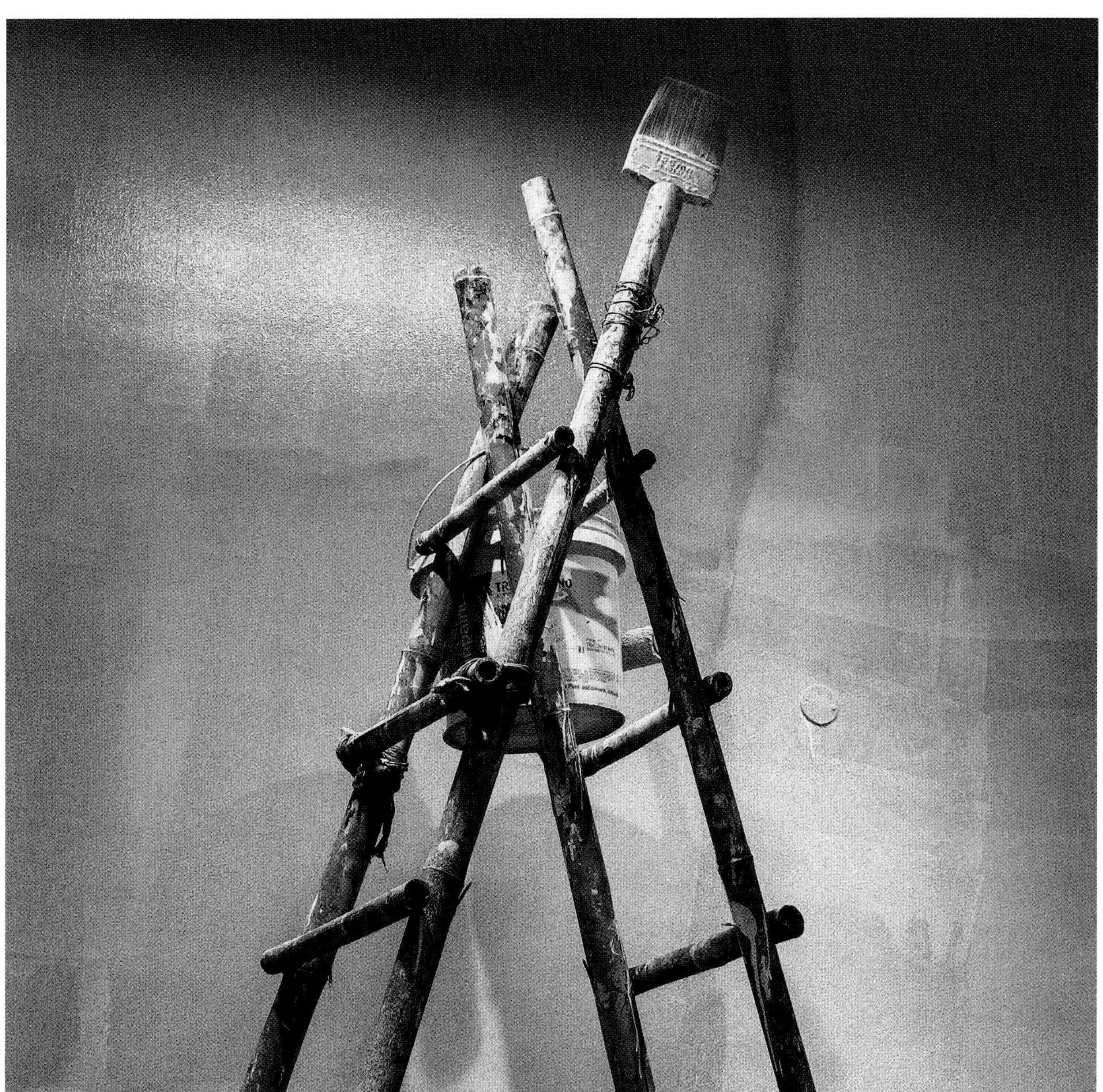

CHAPTER SIX

ART GALLERIES

I cannot recall ever buying art from an art show. I also have seldom been to an art opening. The wine served there is terrible (and they do not serve beer, which is rather ridiculous). I buy all my art online. In spite of having a terrible sense of dimension. But these are some of my go-to-galleries. In several cases, I have been their first buyer which is always a great feeling. The fabulous thing about these galleries is they also showcase young talent which is terribly attractive for me because I think the true trot of buying and selling art is identifying great talent and putting your money behind that. Buying established artists just requires money and no intuition.

”

>

EXPERIMENTER, KOLKATA

>

SHRINE EMPIRE GALLERY, NEW DELHI

>

TARQ, MUMBAI

>

METHOD, MUMBAI

>

NATURE MORTE, NEW DELHI

>

GAGOSIAN, NEW YORK

>

GUGGENHEIM, NEW YORK

>

VENUS OVER MANHATTAN, NEW YORK

>

CHASE CONTEMPORARY, NEW YORK

>

LAURENCE MILLER GALLERY, NEW YORK

>

GREY NOISE, DUBAI

>

TATE MODERN, LONDON

>

HAUSER & WIRTH, LONDON

>

WHITE CUBE, LONDON

>

VAST, THIMPU

>

TRICK EYE MUSEUM, SINGAPORE

>

TANG CONTEMPORARY ART, HONG KONG

>

PRAGUE GALLERY, PRAGUE

>

UFFIZI GALLERY, FLORENCE

>

WEBBER'S, LOS ANGELES

CHAPTER SEVEN

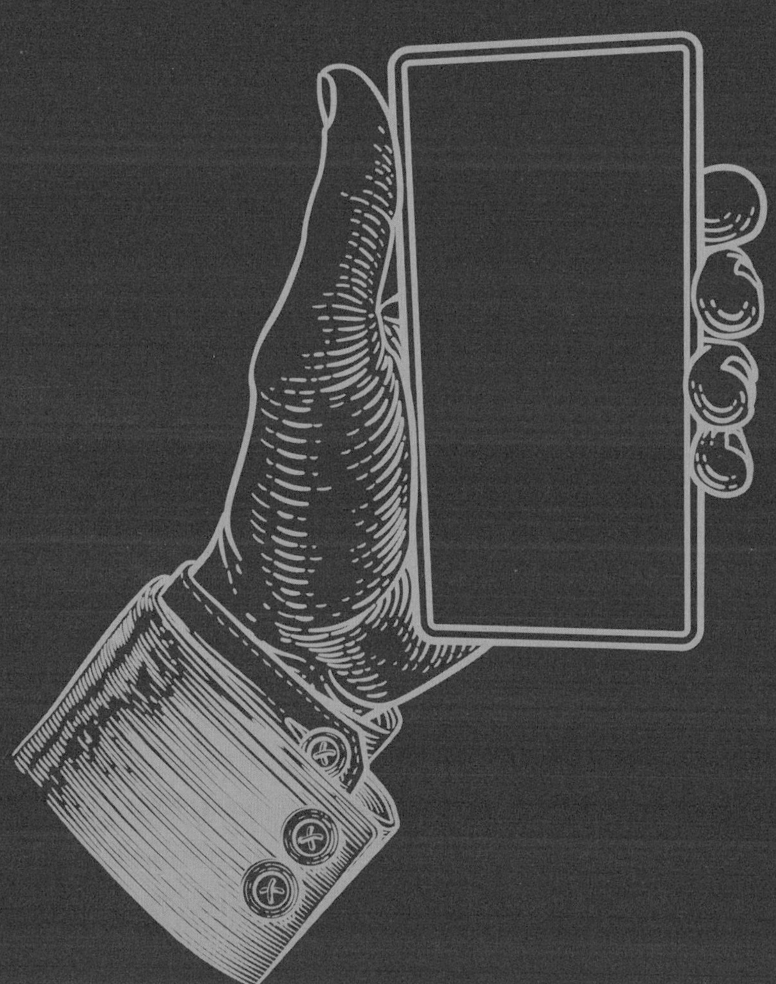

APPS

In terms of technology, I am a tad challenged and blatantly boring. I still prefer my desktop to a laptop or tablet. But when it comes to my apps, I always am on the lookout for cool apps that make my life convenient and cutting-edge. So, I do not use the calendar on my phone. I use Timepage which is a digital version of a Moleskin diary. I stopped printing business cards and have moved to a digital avatar of them called Covve. Tired of the BS that airlines dole out on flight delays, I use Flightradar24 which tells me precisely where my plane is and when will it land. Yet there are few apps on my phone. I believe less is more.

>

TIMEPAGE

>

BLACKLANE

>

CALM

>

COVVE CARD

>

SHAZAM

>

YARN

>

PLANTAPP

>

FLIGHTRADAR24

>

POCKETCASTS

>

LASTPASS

>

MINT

>

INSTASIZE

>

PICMERGER

>

VSCO

>

JUSTFIT

>

DOWN DOG

>

BETTERSLEEP

>

PHOTO VAULT

>

NYT

>

BITE

CHAPTER EIGHT

MUSIC ALBUMS

My taste in music is pendulumlike. It swings from thumri to techno. From soppy pop to achingly wonderful arias. From classical to Japanese jazz. And I am language agnostic. I do not care about the language of the music. Just the vocabulary of its melody. And I Shazam music everywhere I hear it. Which means I have a New York City Cab List of music I heard while travelling in New York cabs. And even my Road List for road trips. Music rejuvenates me and I listen to it by myself every night. Here is my compilation of some cool albums that I heard this year.

”

>

OUR DAILY BREAD BY JOE LOVANO TRIO TAPESTRY

>

I WANT MORE BY DONNY MCCASLIN

>

FROM THE DANCEHALL TO THE BATTLEFIELD BY JASON MORAN

>

PHOENIX BY LAKECIA BENJAMIN

>

EYE OF I BY JAMES BRANDON LEWIS

>

NIELSEN'S SYMPHONIES NOS 2 & 6 BY DANISH NATIONAL SYMPHONY ORCHESTRA/ FABIO LUISI

>

MUSIC FOR STRINGS BY SINFONIA OF LONDON / JOHN WILSON

>

HENSELT COMPLETE ETUDES BY DANIEL GRIMWOOD

>

WOMEN AND WAR AND PEACE BY KATELYN BOUSKA

>

LOST AT SEA BY ROB GRANT

>

UNDERWATER BY LUDOVICO EINAUDI

>

THAT FEELS GOOD BY JESSIE WARE

>

RAVEN BY KALELA

>

BEHIND THE WALLPAPER BY JULIA HOLTER

>

12 BY RYUICHI SAKAMOTO

>

GOOD RIDDANCE BY GRACIE ABRAMS

>

LOVE IN EXILE BY AROOJ AFTAB, VIJAY IYER AND SHAHZAD ISMAILY

>

GAG ORDER BY KESHA

>

DESIRE, I WANT TO TURN INTO YOU BY CAROLINE POLACHECK

>

THE RECORD BY BOYGENIUS

CHAPTER NINE

STOCKS

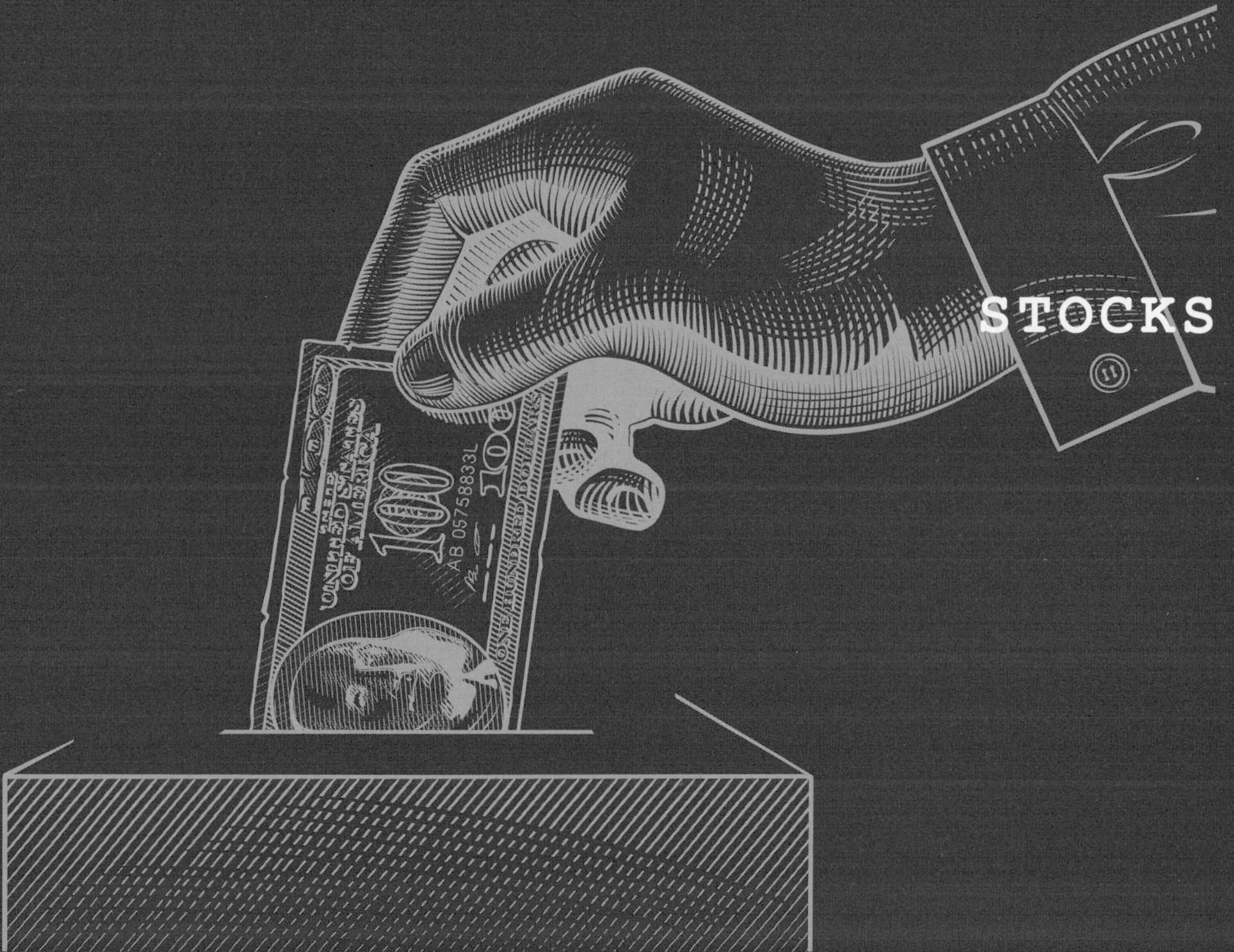

During the pandemic, people learnt how to make sourdough bread. Some learnt a language. Others tended their gardens. I fell in love with stocks and the stock markets. Now the truth of the matter is that I cannot read a screen. Nor do I get P.E. ratios or ROCE or other such vile stuff. I just read and research and then employ my gut feel to pick stocks. My picks largely centre around certain verticals. I focus on AI, gaming, cyber security, mobility, semi-conductors, robotics and healthcare. And my attention is primarily on the U.S. markets. Here is my pick of the ones that do the trick for me.

”

>

ACTIVISION BLIZZARD

>

ADVANCED MICRO DEVICES

>

AMAZON.COM

>

APPLE

>

C3.AI

>

CROWDSTRIKE HOLDINGS

>

GLOBAL X BLOCKCHAIN ETF

>

GLOBAL X ROBOTICS & ARTIFICIAL INTELLIGENCE ETF

>

GUARDANT HEALTH

>

INTUITIVE SURGICAL

>

JPMORGAN CHASE & CO

>

MERCADO LIBRE

>

MICROSOFT

>

MOBILEYE GLOBAL

>

NVIDIA CORPORATION

>

PALANTIR TECHNOLOGIES

>

PALO ALTO NETWORKS

>

SOLAR EDGE TECHNOLOGIES

>

STATE STREET CONSUMER STAPLES ETF

>

VIAST

CHAPTER TEN

GADGETS

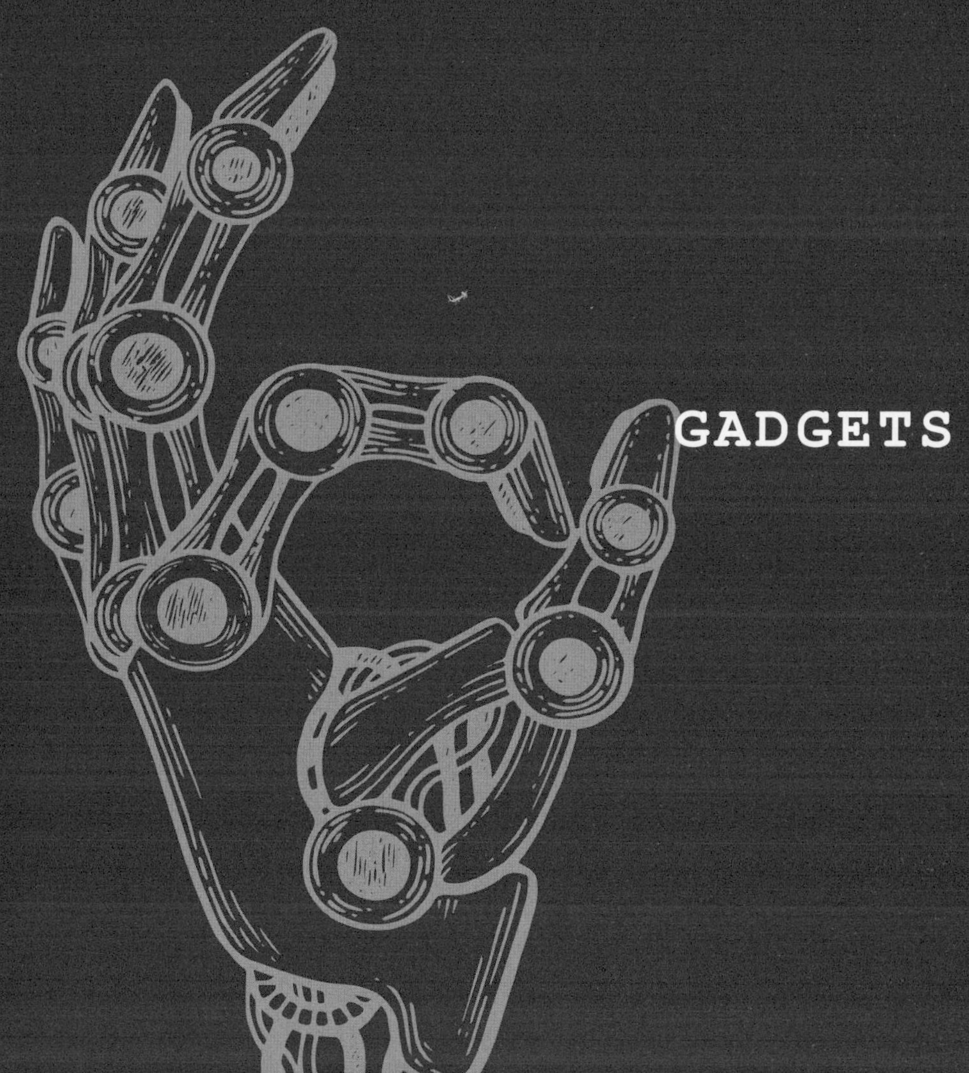

“

I am a great one for gadgets and I use them to better and simplify various facets of my life. They could range from writing gadgets which allow me to type without being distracted by mails or even smart writing sets. They could range from cool headphones to practical yet hip backpacks. And because I smoke, even my air purifier must be just so.

Here is my list of A-list gadgets that I stumbled upon in 2023.

”

>

THE FREEWRITE TRAVELER

>

XTORM SOLAR BOOSTER

>

PROTO'S PHOTO M

>

ROLLING SQUARE'S INCHARGE X

>

WATTR'S CRAZYCAP

>

KIBU HEADPHONES

>

PIEGA MLS 2 GEN2 SPEAKERS

>

MOBVOI TICWATCH PRO 5

>

LEICA Q 3 DIGITAL CAMERA

>

MOLESKINE SMART WRITING SET

>

BARTESIAN COCKTAIL MACHINE

>

TP-LINK ARCHER AX 55 WI-FI ROUTER

>

COWAY AIRMEGA 250 AIR PURIFIER

>

BREVILLE THE SUPER Q BLENDER

>

JBL BAR 1300 X SOUNDBAR

>

FLEXISPOT EN1 STANDING DESK

>

TOM BIHN SYNIK 22 BACKPACK

>

GORUCK SAND KETTLEBAGS

>

PELOTON ORIGINAL BIKE

>

AMAZON ECHO SHOW 10

CHAPTER ELEVEN

FILMS

“

2023 was a terrific year for films. There was “Triangle of Sadness” which is about the lonely lives of supermodels under the farce of the fast life. Also, the gripping “Blackberry” on the phone device that altered almost all our lives and pushed personal productivity to newer boundaries. On a flight to New York, I enjoyed “The Whale”. Evidently amidst a flood of films, I did miss out on several but these count among my favourites for the year.

”

>

TRIANGLE OF SADNESS, RUBEN ÖSTLUND

>

BLACKBERRY, MATTHEW JOHNSON

>

ANATOMY OF A FALL, JUSTINE TRIET

>

FALLEN LEAVES, AKI KAURISMÄKI

>

PERFECT DAYS, WIM WENDERS

>

FIREBRAND, KARIM AÏNOUZ

>

CLUB ZERO, JESSICA HAUSNER

>

A MAN CALLED OTTO, MARC FORSTER

>

MISSING, NICHOLAS D. JOHNSON, WILL MERRICK

>

WHITNEY HOUSTON: I WANNA DANCE WITH SOMEBODY, KASI LEMMONS

>

THE MAGICIAN'S ELEPHANT, WENDY ROGERS

>

THE SON, FLORIAN ZELLER

>

SR., CHRIS SMITH

>

STUZ, JONAH HILL

>

FOOL'S PARADISE, CHARLIE DAY

>

THE STRAYS, NATHANIEL MARTELLO-WHITE

>

THE UNFORGIVABLE, NORA FINGSCHEIDT

>

THE WHALE, DARREN ARONOFSKY

>

SHE SAID, MARIA SCHRADER

>

CHAPTER TWELVE

TV SERIES

There is no denying that after the discovery of electricity, OTT has been mankind’s greatest discovery. The pandemic also weaned us away from cinema halls and brought great content to our tablets and TVs. This year, President Barack Obama led the show as far as TV series were concerned with two great shows: “Working: What we do all day”. And “Our Great National Parks”. But there was more. A riveting season of “Succession”. A great series on tennis-”Break Point”. And a bunch of other fantastic stuff. Do watch.

”

>

CLASS OF '09

>

SUCCESSION: SEASON 4

>

JURY DUTY

>

SHRINKING

>

HAPPY VALLEY: SEASON 3

>

A SMALL LIGHT

>

BEEF: SEASON 1

>

THE TRAITORS: SEASON 1

>

PLATONIC : SEASON 1

>

A SPY AMONG FRIENDS

>

PRETTY BABY: BROOKE SHIELDS: SEASON I

>

TRUE LIES: SEASON I

>

BLUE LIGHTS

>

THE CROWDED ROOM: SEASON I

>

WHITE HOUSE PLUMBERS

>

YOUR HONOR

>

WORKING: WHAT WE DO ALL DAY

>

BREAK POINT

>

OUR GREAT NATIONAL PARKS

>

CRUEL SUMMER

chris evans
know your medical options
INTELLIGENCE BEYOND THOUGHT

CHAPTER THIRTEEN

BOOKS

“

I read a book a day. You read that right. I derive immense inspiration from them. But I have one rule-I never read fiction. Never have. Many have called that a character flaw but so be it. 2023 was pregnant with brilliant books. I read all kinds of subjects: because I do not exercise, I read on health and hacks that can improve it. I read a lot of business, several memoirs, books on chips, cricket and even consulting.

”

>

HACKING HEALTH, MUKESH BANSAL

>

OUTLIVE, BILL GIFFORD AND PETER ATTIA

>

NEVER FINISHED, DAVID GOGGINS

>

THE BIG BULL OF DALAL STREET, NEIL BORATE

>

ELIZABETH: AN INTIMATE PORTRAIT, GYLES BRANDRETH

>

SULTAN: A MEMOIR, GIDEON HAIGH AND WASEEM AKRAM

>

UP CLOSE AND ALL IN, JOHN E. MACK

>

THE SUCCESSOR, PADDY MANNING

>

CHIP WAR, CHRIS MILLER

>

THE POWER LAW, SEBASTIAN MALLABY

>

WHEN MCKINSEY COMES TO TOWN, WALT BOGDANICH AND MICHAEL FORSYTH

>

TRAITOR KING, ANDREW LOWNIE

>

REBEL KING, TOM BOWER

>

THE CRYPTOPIANS, LAURA SHIN

>

WHEN THINGS FALL APART, PEMA CHÖDRÖN

>

AFTERNESS, ASHOK GANGULY

>

WHY ZEBRAS DON'T GET ULCERS, ROBERT M. SAPOLSKY

>

90 DAYS, ANIRUDHYA MITRA

>

SOLI SORABJEE: LIFE AND TIMES, ABHINAV CHANDRACHUD

>

GRIT, ANGELA DUCKWORTH

CHAPTER FOURTEEN

WEBSITES

I am socially challenged and step out in the evenings 14 days a year. The rest of the time, I enjoy being on the net. It helps me realize my daily goal of learning three new things. Now, make no mistake, I do not aimlessly surf the net. I have a variety of interests: advertising, stock markets, design, wines, music, opinions. So, I have a stack of websites that I go to every evening from 7-9 pm. For me it is the ultimate form of both relaxation and education. And it fuels my curiousity which is my single reason to exist.

>

READCEREAL.COM

>

FT.COM

>

WIRED.COM

>

WALLPAPER.COM

>

CNTRAVELLER.COM

>

LONGFORM.ORG

>

THEBROWSER.COM

>

GETPOCKET.COM

>

NYT.COM

>

WSJ.COM

>

KICKSTARTER.COM

>

TRENDERA.COM

>

POETRY.ORG

>

DELISH.COM

>

MOMA.ORG

>

REFINETHEMIND.TUMBLR.COM

>

THECOOLHUNTER.NET

>

FOOL.COM

>

MONOCLE.COM

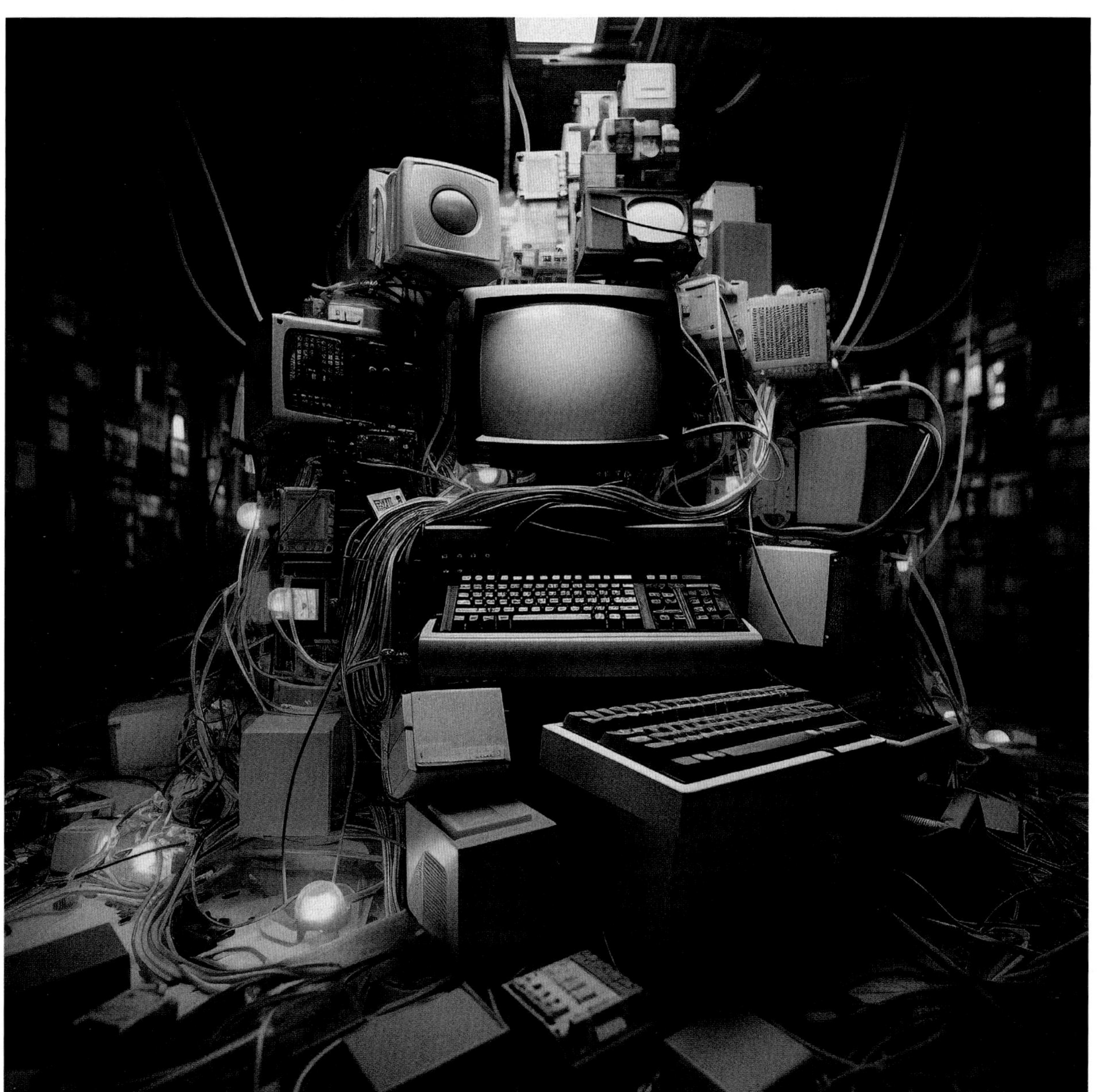

CHAPTER FIFTEEN

FRAGRANCES

“

Fragrances define my life. They serve as a sensorial compass for my day. Right from my shower gel to my deo down to the fragrance in my car or my candle in the workplace. Fragrances design and determine my mood and attitude. I take great pains to select the fragrance in the workplace, as much as I do for the bedroom. Here are my coolest whiffs and sniffs.

>

SANTA MARIA NOVELLA TABACCO TOSCANO

>

EIGHT & BOB

>

MALIN + GOETZE OTTO CANDLE

>

BYREDO SUEDE

>

YSL KOUROS

>

PENHALIGON'S JUNIPER SLING

>

THE TEA PARTY

>

TRVDON CARMELITE

>

BULY 1803 SAVON SUPERFIN MEDINA OUD

>

HOTEL COSTES BROWN SCENTED CANDLE

>

CLAUS PORTO CHYPRE CEDAR POINSETTIA

>

DIPTYQUE EAU DE LIERRE

>

UNIVERSAL SOUL STILL

>

NASOMATTO DURO

>

MILLER HARRIS PEAU SANTAL

>

COUTO TOOTHPASTE

>

LEATHER EAU DE PARFUM ACQUA DI PARMA

>

EAU D'ITALIE SCENTED CANDLE

>

JO MALONE LONDON ENGLISH PEAR & FREESIA

>

CREED AVENTUS

COSTES

SWAPAN SETH is a columnist, an advertising and marketing professional, a corporate speaker, a tastemaker and trend-spotter. He is also the author of the best-selling THIS IS ALL I HAVE TO SAY. Swapan collects books, paper, inks and wines. He lives in Gurgaon with his wife and two sons.